COUNTERING al Qaeda

An Appreciation of the Situation and Suggestions for Strategy

Brian Michael Jenkins

RAND

This publication was supported by RAND using its own funds.

Library of Congress Cataloging-in-Publication Data

Jenkins, Brian Michael.
    Countering Al Qaeda : an appreciation of the situation and suggestions for
strategy / Brian Michael Jenkins.
        p. cm.
    Includes bibliographical references.
    "MR-1620."
    ISBN 0-8330-3264-X (pbk.)
    1. War on Terrorism, 2001– 2. Qaida (Organization) 3. Terrorism. 4. United
States—Military policy. 5. Terrorism—Government policy—United States. I. Rand
Corporation. II.Title.

    HV6432.7 .J46 2002
    363.3'2'0973—dc21
                                                                    2002012737

RAND is a nonprofit institution that helps improve policy and decisionmaking through research and analysis. RAND® is a registered trademark. RAND's publications do not necessarily reflect the opinions or policies of its research sponsors.

Cover design by Maritta Tapanainen

Published 2002 by RAND
1700 Main Street, P.O. Box 2138, Santa Monica, CA 90407-2138
1200 South Hayes Street, Arlington, VA 22202-5050
201 North Craig Street, Suite 202, Pittsburgh, PA 15213-1516
RAND URL: http://www.rand.org/
To order RAND documents or to obtain additional information,
contact Distribution Services: Telephone: (310) 451-7002;
Fax: (310) 451-6915; Email: order@rand.org

PREFACE

This monograph grew out of several briefings. Subsequent to the briefings, the work was substantially extended and updated to reflect later developments. Support for writing this monograph was provided by RAND, using its corporate funds.

Comments are welcome and may be addressed to the author:

Brian M. Jenkins
RAND
P.O. Box 2138
Santa Monica, CA 90407-2138
Brian_Jenkins@rand.org

CONTENTS

Preface   iii

Summary   vii

Acknowledgments   xi

Chapter One
    INTRODUCTION   1

Chapter Two
    UNDERSTANDING THE ENEMY   3
    The Emergence of al Qaeda   3
    Process, Planning, and Mission   4
    Changed Perceptions of the Terrorist Threat   6
    The Aftermath of September 11: al Qaeda's View   7
    Some Realistic Assumptions   15

Chapter Three
    STRATEGY FOR THE SECOND PHASE OF THE WAR
    ON TERRORISM   17

SUMMARY

Since the terrorist attacks of September 11, 2001, the United States has achieved significant successes in its war on terrorism. Removing the Taliban government in Afghanistan, thereby eliminating al Qaeda's sanctuary and training camps, has broken an important link in the process that once provided al Qaeda's leadership with a continuing flow of recruits. Toppling the Taliban also demonstrated American resolve and international support, and it underscored the considerable risk run by governments that provide assistance to terrorists.

Having achieved its initial goals in Afghanistan, the United States is now in a second, more complex phase of the war, where it must continue its efforts to destroy al Qaeda and at the same time attempt to combat terrorism as a mode of conflict. Al Qaeda, along with its associates and its successors, will fight on, drawing upon a deep reservoir of hatred and a desire for revenge. It must be presumed that al Qaeda will exploit all of its ability to cause catastrophic death and destruction—there will be no self-imposed limits to its violence. It can also be presumed that the organization will continue its efforts to acquire and use weapons of mass destruction (WMD); that it will attack U.S. targets abroad where possible; and that it will attempt to mount attacks within the United States. Al Qaeda constitutes the most serious immediate threat to the security of the United States.

Although some measure of success has been achieved in uncovering terrorist plots, the ability of U.S. agencies to detect and prevent future terrorist attacks is limited. Al Qaeda, however, must now operate in a less-permissive environment. If al Qaeda can be kept on the run, the numbers it can train will decline. And declining numbers eventually will result in a corresponding qualitative decline in terrorist operations. However, it is possible that al Qaeda will adapt to the more difficult post-September 11 operational environment by morphing into an even looser network, devolving more initiative and resources to local operatives.

The greatest challenge in the second phase of the campaign against terrorism is that as military operations move beyond a single theater, the more complex tasks will be dispersed among numerous departments, agencies, and offices, and the focus on the overall U.S. strategy will be lost, along with the nation's ability to coordinate operations. The American campaign must continue to emphasize the following central elements:

- The destruction of al Qaeda remains the primary aim.

- The pursuit of al Qaeda must be single-minded and unrelenting.

- The campaign against terrorism will take time, possibly decades.

- The fight in Afghanistan must be continued as long as al Qaeda operatives remain in the country.

- Pakistan must be kept on the side of the allies in efforts to destroy the remnants of al Qaeda and the Taliban and dilute Islamic extremism.

- New networks must be created to exploit intelligence across frontiers.

- The goals of the war on terrorism cannot be accomplished unilaterally—international cooperation is a prerequisite for success.

- This is a war against specific terrorists, the larger goal of which is to combat terrorism.

- The strategy should include political warfare, aimed at reducing the appeal of extremists, encouraging alternative views, and discouraging terrorists' use of WMD.

- Deterrent strategies may be appropriate for dealing with the terrorists' support structures.

- It must be made clear that terrorist use of WMD will bring extraordinary responses.

- Homeland security strategies must be developed that are both effective and efficient.

- The war against the terrorists at home and abroad must be conducted in a way that is consistent with American values.

Finally, it is necessary to be determinedly pragmatic. America's goal is not revenge for the September 11 attacks. The goal is not even bringing individual terrorists to justice. It is the destruction of a terrorist enterprise that threatens American security and, by extension, the security of the world.

ACKNOWLEDGMENTS

The author would like to thank Paul Davis for the stimulating debates that propelled earlier briefings into this essay; Ambassador L. Paul Bremer III for his thoughtful review and remarks; and finally, Janet DeLand for her useful comments and skillful editing.

Chapter One

INTRODUCTION

Since the terrorist attacks of September 11, 2001, the United States has achieved significant successes in its war on terrorism. Removing the Taliban government in Afghanistan, thereby eliminating al Qaeda's sanctuary and training camps, has broken an important link in the process that once provided al Qaeda's leadership with a continuing flow of recruits. Toppling the Taliban also demonstrated American resolve and international support, and it underscored the considerable risk run by governments that provide assistance to terrorists.

The United States has avoided portraying its campaign against al Qaeda and the Taliban as a crusade against Islam (an accusation made by al Qaeda's leaders), and it has successfully brought about a fundamental change in Pakistan's policy. Once a Taliban supporter, Pakistan has become an ally in the campaign against Islamic extremism. U.S. diplomacy has also turned the international outrage and concern prompted by the September 11 attacks into a global commitment to combat terrorism, confirmed in United Nations Resolution 1373. Through its military presence in Uzbekistan, its diplomatic intervention in the confrontation between Pakistan and India over Kashmir, and its direct military assistance to the Philippines and Georgia, the United States has limited al Qaeda's ability to exploit other conflicts and develop new bases.

Despite these successes, the United States still faces a serious terrorist threat. Public warnings of possible attacks continue to rattle nerves and impede economic recovery, and September 11 signaled a fundamental and permanent change in the security environment.

But while Americans are apprehensive, still in shock over the attacks on the World Trade Center and the Pentagon, they appear reluctant to accept that this was not a one-time anomaly. Despite the continuing issuance of new warnings, Americans are capable of lapsing into a dangerous complacency.

The tasks of reorganizing government, investigating perceived failures in intelligence, implementing new security measures, dealing with new crises abroad, and addressing important domestic matters inevitably distract government and public attention from the very real threat posed by al Qaeda. In this environment, one can understand the relentless determination of the otherwise unappealing ancient Roman Senator Cato, who reportedly concluded every speech with the reminder that "Carthage must be destroyed."

Having achieved its initial goals in Afghanistan, the United States is now in a second, more complex phase of the war, where it must continue its efforts to destroy al Qaeda and at the same time attempt to combat terrorism as a mode of conflict. This will require the orchestration of intelligence collection, the pursuit of traditional criminal investigations leading to trials, the imposition of financial controls and economic sanctions as well as offers of material reward, the application of conventional military power, the use of covert and special operations, the provision of military assistance, and psychological warfare to disrupt terrorist operations and destroy terrorist groups. Greater international coordination will be required. Without a clear exposition of strategy, the focus of the campaign could easily be lost.

Chapter Two

UNDERSTANDING THE ENEMY

THE EMERGENCE OF AL QAEDA

Al Qaeda was a product of the struggle to eject the Soviet Union from Afghanistan. Portrayed as a holy war, that campaign brought together volunteers and financial contributors from throughout the Islamic world. Muslims from Algeria, Egypt, Saudi Arabia, Southeast Asia, and beyond fought side by side, forging relationships and creating a cadre of veterans who shared a powerful life experience, a more global view, and a heady sense of confidence underscored by the Soviet Union's ultimate withdrawal and subsequent collapse, for which they assumed credit. Instead of being welcomed home as heroes, however, the returning veterans of the Afghan campaign were watched by suspicious regimes who worried that the religious fervor of the fighters posed a political threat. Isolated at home, they became ready recruits for new campaigns.

There were ample reasons and opportunities to continue the fight: the Gulf War and the consequent arrival of American troops in Saudi Arabia; the continued repression of Islamic challenges to local regimes; armed struggles in Algeria, Egypt, the newly independent Muslim republics of the former Soviet Union, Kashmir, the Philippines, and Bosnia; the forces of globalization that seemed threatening to all local cultures; and the continuing civil war in Afghanistan. Organizational survival, the natural desire to continue in meaningful activity, and the rewards of status and an inflated self-image contributed powerful incentives to continue the fight. The subsequent victories of a like-minded Taliban guaranteed safe haven for the militants and their training camps, which graduated thousands of additional volunteers.

What Osama bin Laden and his associates contributed to this potent but unfocused force was a sense of vision, mission, and strategy that combined 20th century theory of a unified Islamic polity with restoration of the Islamic Caliphate that, at its height, stretched from Spain to India. This vision had operational utility. It recast the numerous local conflicts into a single struggle between an authentic Islam and a host of corrupt satraps who would collapse without the backing of the West—the United States in particular. It thereby provided a single, easily agreed-upon enemy, whose fate, when confronted with a unified Islamic struggle, would be the same as that of the Soviet Union. By erasing the boundaries between individual countries and their conflicts, al Qaeda could draw upon a much larger reservoir of human resources for the larger battle. In addition to the thousands of veterans of the war against the Soviet Union, al Qaeda now had thousands of new recruits to train.

Quantity ultimately translates into quality. It enables organizers to identify and exploit specialized talent that would be scarce or not available in a smaller enterprise. This is key to al Qaeda's operational capabilities. Amply funded, protected in Afghanistan, supported by Pakistan, motivated by a powerful vision, al Qaeda became the banner carrier of Islam's response to past defeats, frustration, humiliation, resentment, and fear. Al Qaeda's spectacular terrorist blows against the United States in Africa and the Middle East and America's feeble response, despite its vigorous denunciations, made Osama bin Laden a heroic leader. Everything seemed to confirm al Qaeda's calculations.

PROCESS, PLANNING, AND MISSION

Al Qaeda is more than just an organization; it is also a process, and its principal resource is its human capital. Al Qaeda's future ability to grow and continue operations depends most strongly on its ability to gather new recruits.

On the basis of what we know about the September 11 attackers and the limited testimony of captured al Qaeda operatives, al Qaeda appears to function like many cults. Frustrated immigrants in Europe and America, drifters living on the margins of society, seekers of absolute truth or greater meaning in their lives, lonely souls with varying levels of education show up—on their own or invited by friends—at mosques and prayer groups, a few of which offer radical interpretations of faith. Fiery sermons identify common enemies, the obstacles to political and personal achievement. Recruiters watch for resonance and select promising acolytes for more intense indoctrination and training.

Prior to September 11, the training camps in Afghanistan provided a way of testing commitment. In Afghanistan, volunteers faced hardship and sacrifice, as well as opportunities for combat. With practical training came further indoctrination. The recruits became part of a secret international brotherhood that superseded all other affiliations and loyalties.

Fulfillment of the radical Islamic vision of heroic deeds leading to the restoration of a utopian Islamic empire on earth—or, if God wills, eternal reward in the hereafter—requires embracing an aggressive interpretation of jihad. Exhortations to kill in quantity underscore the teaching that there are no innocents in this war. The most intelligent and dedicated volunteers receive further training and indoctrination, and they return to the world with a sense of mission and power. Of course, not all are Mohammed Attas, fanatics capable of planning and executing complex operations. Some are "acorns," buried at random to be dug up when needed for an operation.

Most of the proposals for terrorist operations appear to come from the operatives in the field, rather than from the center. Approval from above, however, brings resources that elevate such plans to a deadlier realm. The provision of technical advice, money, documents, and additional manpower to the self-selected warriors suggests the existence of an underground bureaucracy—al Qaeda has middle management. Some operations seem to receive little central support, but a plan for an attack on the scale of September 11 would certainly have significant central control and could well have been initiated by al Qaeda's command.

An attack that carries the al Qaeda brand, duly credited in the news media to Osama bin Laden, thus enhances his reputation. Each attack becomes a recruiting poster, demonstrating the power of al Qaeda's interpretation of Islam, attracting more recruits.

CHANGED PERCEPTIONS OF THE TERRORIST THREAT

The September 11 attack destroyed America's sense of invulnerability and illustrated the limits of its intelligence infrastructure. It demonstrated that foreign terrorists were capable of mounting major attacks on U.S. soil without being detected. Preparations for earlier terrorist attacks, including the 1996 bombing of Khobar Towers in Saudi Arabia, the bombings of the American embassies in Kenya and Tanzania, and the attack on the U.S.S. Cole, had also gone undetected, but those incidents took place in areas where U.S. authorities had limited opportunities to obtain intelligence firsthand. Preparations for the 1993 bombing of the World Trade Center and the 1995 bombing of the federal building in Oklahoma City had also gone undetected, but these were the work of small domestic conspiracies (although there was some foreign participation in the 1993 World Trade Center bombing). The fact that at least 20 operatives from a terrorist organization that was already being closely watched by American intelligence services could enter the United States, remain in the country for months while training to carry out multiple terrorist attacks of unprecedented scale, receive instructions and hundreds of thousands of dollars from abroad, even travel out of the country and return, all without being detected by the authorities, raised questions about the adequacy of American intelligence that are still being debated.

September 11 also raised the lethality of terrorism to a new level. The terrorists clearly were determined to cause catastrophic casualties— tens of thousands of casualties—confirming a long-term trend toward increasingly large-scale, indiscriminate attacks. Tens died in the worst incidents of terrorism in the 1970s, hundreds in the 1980s and 1990s, but thousands died on September 11. The September 11 attacks involved an imaginative plan (although no exotic weapons), and they indicated a mindset that would not preclude the use of weapons of mass destruction (WMD) if the terrorists could somehow acquire them. Subsequent discoveries in al Qaeda's training camps showed that the use of chemical, biological, and nuclear weapons certainly was an aspiration, even if the organization lacked the actual capabilities.

Fears of bioterrorism increased when a still unidentified perpetrator sent letters contaminated with anthrax to target recipients in the news media and government. No evidence directly connects the anthrax attacks to al Qaeda's September 11 attack, but the coincidence in timing led to a convergence of concerns. Regardless of who was responsible for the anthrax attacks, bioterrorism had become a deadly and disruptive reality.

THE AFTERMATH OF SEPTEMBER 11: AL QAEDA'S VIEW

From the terrorists' perspective, the September 11 attacks dealt a massive blow to the most prominent symbols of American economic and military might, a dramatic demonstration of what could be achieved through commitment to the Islamic extremists' vision of jihad. Al Qaeda's leadership probably anticipated that the attack would provoke a major military response, which it could then portray as an assault on Islam. This would inspire thousands of additional volunteers and could provoke the entire Islamic world to rise up against the West. Governments that opposed the people's wrath, quislings to Western imperialism, would fall. The West would be destroyed.

If this was al Qaeda's rapture, it repeated the folly of terrorists past. The strategy of carrying out spectacular attacks to deliberately provoke an overreaction by government authorities which, in turn, would provoke a popular uprising has seldom worked, and it didn't work this time either. To be sure, the attacks on the World Trade Center and the Pentagon were popular on Arab streets, where they were met with spontaneous celebrations and reportedly made Osama a popular name for new babies. But when the United States launched its attack on Afghanistan, careful not to portray it as an assault on Islam despite bin Laden's efforts to do so, there were no visible rivers of recruits streaming toward al Qaeda's banner, nor were there any uprisings or organized resistance.

More than nine months after the attacks, the Taliban have been removed from government, although not eliminated from Afghanistan entirely, and al Qaeda has lost its sanctuary and training camps. The "business continuity" plans that al Qaeda probably had in place before September 11 may have permitted many of its leaders and operatives to escape, but some have been killed, others have been captured, and the rest are on the run. Pakistan, once a source of support and recruits, has reversed its policy and cracked down on Taliban and al Qaeda sympathizers. Other governments in the Middle East and beyond have rounded up al Qaeda suspects and have committed themselves to cooperation in combating terrorism, although they still cannot agree on a definition of what terrorism is. Whatever appreciation Palestinians might have owed Osama bin Laden for opportunistically including their cause on his broader agenda has been offset by the vicissitudes of their own struggle. Its operatives forced deeper underground and its financial supporters forced to be more circumspect, al Qaeda's balance sheet does not look so favorable. However, we have not seen the last of al Qaeda.

Al Qaeda will not quit. Terrorist groups seldom quit, and al Qaeda did not retire on September 12. Growing evidence acquired since September 11 suggests that in addition to taking steps to protect its finances, instructing some of its key operatives to disappear, and making preparations to protect its leadership, Al Qaeda has vowed to carry out further attacks. And indeed, terrorist attacks have occurred in Pakistan, Tunisia, and Saudi Arabia, and other terrorist plots have been discovered before they could be carried out. Some of the plots originated prior to September 11, but others were set in motion afterwards. Not all of the plots are directly linked to al Qaeda, although some clearly are. Some of the attacks may have simply been provoked by America's war on terrorism and Pakistan's decision to support it, as well as by other events in the Middle East.

Al Qaeda's leaders may have underestimated the American response, just as they may have overestimated the readiness of their sympathizers to rise up against the West. They now must adapt their organization and strategy to this new reality, but they will continue their campaign.

Religious conviction gives them strength, but the armed struggle is what holds them together. Violence is their *raison d'être*. The enterprise of terrorism provides status, power, and psychological satisfaction. It attracts new recruits. It demonstrates their devotion and gives them historical importance. Without terrorism, al Qaeda would collapse into just another exotic sect.

Terrorists understand when they suffer setbacks, but they operate in a clandestine world, a closed universe cut off from normal discourse and competing views. They measure success differently: They define death and destruction as achievements in themselves. Terrorists do not feel that it is necessary to translate these into political progress, and they have a high tolerance for cognitive dissonance. Adversity is seen as a test of their commitment. Compromise equals apostasy, so leaders counseling restraint risk accusations of betrayal. In an association of extremists, it is perilous to be less than the most extreme. Successes are seen to derive from violence, and setbacks thus call for greater violence. Individual terrorists may become disillusioned, but there is no easy way for them to leave the organization. A few groups have officially suspended their campaigns of violence, but their leaders were denounced, while splinter and rival groups vowed to fight on.

Other groups have faded with the death or capture of charismatic and effective leaders (e.g., Peru's Shining Path and Turkey's PKK), the loss of state sponsors or the imposition of state control which left their tongues but removed their teeth (the Palestinian rejectionists currently residing in Damascus), or the drying up of their reservoir of support (America's Weather Underground). In some cases, circumstances changed, making the terrorists' struggle less relevant (e.g., Germany's Red Army Faction). Other groups have disappeared when a generation passed without successors. The evolution of terrorist organizations is a long process, measured in decades.

Sources of al Qaeda's strength. Although al Qaeda has been damaged by the American-led campaign, it continues to benefit from its image as a powerful Islamic force that is capable of inflicting devastating blows on its foes. Osama bin Laden's mystique survives, even if his personal fate is in doubt. Al Qaeda's key figures remain at large, and there may be others who have not yet been identified.

It is more difficult to assess the capability of al Qaeda's global network. We know that as of September 11, 2001, it was extensive, reportedly in place in at least 60 countries. More than 2,000 suspected al Qaeda operatives have been captured or arrested, but others have disappeared underground. Since September 11, terrorist attacks carried out or thwarted in Singapore, Pakistan, Saudi Arabia, Lebanon, Tunisia, Morocco, Macedonia, Bosnia, Italy, France, and the United States indicate that al Qaeda's operational capability still exists. It is able to communicate, reconnoiter targets, plan operations, travel, meet clandestinely, and obtain finances.

Al Qaeda also still benefits from a large reservoir of recruits. While many have been dispersed or perhaps temporarily demoralized, at least some fighters remain dedicated and willing to carry out attacks, including suicide missions. That some attacks have been prevented by intelligence, alert police, or simply good luck is fortunate. At the same time, there remains the nagging fear that another catastrophic attack is being prepared somewhere and that it will be revealed only when it occurs, days, months, or years from now.

Terrorist organizations benefit from having virtually unlimited targets, as homeland defense planners are discovering. Al Qaeda's strategy playbook, however, shows certain preferences. Commercial aviation, diplomatic facilities, and American (or allied) servicemen recur as targets. Naval vessels in port (or in narrow straits), government buildings, monuments, and symbolic landmarks also figure prominently. Finally, al Qaeda enjoys a large constituency that accepts and applauds extreme violence against the West in general and the United States in particular.

Operating environment. While al Qaeda clearly continues to benefit from certain strengths, it must now operate in a less-permissive environment. The loss of the supportive Taliban government, its easily accessible safe haven, and its training camps may not be felt immediately, as al Qaeda will be able to draw upon its reserves for some time while it tries to establish new centers. But these are likely to be smaller and less accessible. Moreover, the pilgrimage to Afghanistan, the experience in the training camps, and participation in Afghanistan's armed conflict served an important role in attracting and indoctrinating volunteers to the cause and in providing future terrorist operatives. Televised videotapes and virtual realms on the Internet may not suffice to maintain a high level of devotion. If al Qaeda can be kept on the run, the numbers it can train will decline. And declining numbers eventually will result in a corresponding qualitative decline in terrorist operations.

Pakistan's withdrawal of support for the Taliban and its promised crackdown on the extremist religious schools that supplied volunteers for al Qaeda's training camps will also reduce the flow of recruits. Poorly educated Pakistani youth were never likely to become sophisticated international operatives. On the other hand, they will pose a continuing danger within Pakistan.

Financial contributors may also be constrained by international efforts to limit terrorist finances. The new measures will not prevent the financing of terrorist operations, which require relatively small amounts, but they could reduce al Qaeda's welfare and proselytizing efforts. The new laws also provide additional sources of intelligence about terrorist organizations.

Finally, increased surveillance and intelligence gathered from captured al Qaeda members and documents will further increase al Qaeda's risks.

Adapting to new circumstances. The greatest threat posed by al Qaeda is that it will attempt another attack as catastrophic as the September 11 attacks or even more so. None of the terrorist plots uncovered since then have been that ambitious, but we know now that the planning for the September 11 attacks was under way for several years, overlapping planning for other major attacks and undetected by the authorities.

An attack on the scale of September 11 could have profound political, social, and economic consequences for the United States. It could inspire widespread anxiety, anger at the government for failing in its primary mission of providing security, and popular demand for draconian measures that could shake the American political system and fundamentally alter the American lifestyle. The economic effects of such an attack, the subsequent disruption, and the need for even greater security measures could be devastating to the economy. But that level of destruction can be achieved only with coordinated conventional attacks, multidimensional assaults calculated to magnify the disruption, or the use of chemical, biological, or nuclear weapons. These, in turn, are likely to need the kind of organization that requires some participation on the part of al Qaeda's central command. We are uncertain whether al Qaeda's key leaders are still alive or able to "do" strategy. Wild-eyed recruits may be plentiful.

Brains are precious. Thus, the immediate goal of the war on terrorism must be to destroy al Qaeda's ability to operate at this level.

It is also possible that al Qaeda will adapt to the more difficult post-September 11 operational environment by morphing into an even looser network, devolving more initiative and resources to local operatives. This does not appear to be inconsistent with al Qaeda's current operational philosophy, which seems to invite local initiative. A looser al Qaeda network would be better able to survive the intense worldwide surveillance of authorities, but it might not be able to operate at the level required for a catastrophic attack. The failed attempt to sabotage an American airliner last December might be characteristic of this level of organization.

Continuing, but uncoordinated, acts of terrorism may be waged by al Qaeda cells, unconnected supporters, and even individuals, inspired by al Qaeda's call or provoked by America's war on terrorism. It may be difficult to distinguish these from isolated acts of violence unconnected with any terrorist organization. Such attacks could be lethal and capable of inspiring terror among an already apprehensive population, but they are likely to remain sporadic events. The anthrax letters and the recent bombings in Pakistan are characteristic of this level of terrorism.

Prospects for the use of weapons of mass destruction. Much of the concern about the current terrorist threat relates to the possible employment of WMD. These include chemical and biological weapons, radioactive dispersal devices, and, potentially, stolen nuclear weapons or improvised nuclear devices. Such concerns are not new; they have been debated at least since the early 1970s.[1] Participants in that debate could appropriately be described in theological terms, since the arguments reflected beliefs more than evidence. "Apocalyptians" believed that terrorist escalation to mass destruction was inevitable, while disbelievers pointed to the absence of any evidence indicating that terrorists were moving in this direction. In the middle were "prudent agnostics," who remained uncertain about whether chemical, biological, or nuclear terrorism was inevitable but nonetheless argued for increased security.

---

[1] I wrote my first monograph on the topic in 1974 (see Brian Michael Jenkins, *Will Terrorists Go Nuclear?* Santa Monica, CA: RAND, P-5541, 1975).

Skeptics found support in the fact that terrorists at that time clearly did not operate at the upper limits of their capabilities if mayhem was their goal. Terrorists who did not understand technically challenging chemical, biological, or nuclear weapons certainly knew how to build large conventional bombs, which they could have set off in public areas to kill far more people than they did. The fact that they did not do so, therefore, had to indicate that they operated under self-imposed constraints. Subsequent research showed that terrorists argued about the proper level of violence. Some believed that wanton killing could jeopardize group cohesion. They also did not want to alienate their perceived legions of supporters. Terrorists wanted publicity and to create alarm; they did not necessarily want to provoke public backlashes that would support government crackdowns that the terrorists themselves might not survive.

In the 1980s, the constraints appeared to erode as terrorists escalated their violence, especially in the Middle East. By the 1990s, terrorists turned to large-scale, indiscriminate attacks calculated to kill in quantity. Part—but only part—of the reason could be found in the changing motives that drove conflict in the final decade of the 20th century. Whereas terrorism in the 1970s and 1980s had been driven mostly by political ideology—terrorists had secular motives, political agendas, and therefore constituents, real or imaginary, on whose behalf they fought—terrorism in the 1990s was increasingly driven by ideologies that exploited religion. The conviction that they had God's sanction freed religious fanatics from ordinary political or moral constraints. But the religious angle should not be overstated, as some of the most deadly terrorist attacks, in terms of fatalities, were carried out by agents of Libya, who sabotaged PanAm and UTA flights in 1988 and 1989, or North Koreans, who brought down a Korean airliner in 1987. Nor should the frequency of large-scale attacks be overestimated. According to RAND's chronology of international terrorism, between 1968 and September 11, 2001, only 14 of more than 10,000 international terrorist incidents resulted in 100 or more fatalities, although there appear to have been more attempts to kill in quantity.

At the same time the terrorists seemed to be escalating their violence, the fall of the Soviet Union raised concerns about the security of the Soviet weapons research program and its vast nuclear arsenal. In an environment of poverty, increasing corruption, and growing organized crime, would Soviet weapons remain secure? Would impoverished Soviet weapons designers and builders find employment in the clandestine weapons research programs of would-be proliferators or state sponsors of terrorism? Might Russia or other republics of the former Soviet Union, desperate for hard currency, willingly provide the materiel and expertise that could accelerate nuclear weapons development by terrorist organizations? Further anxiety derived from the realization that Iraq was further along in developing WMD than had been imagined.

The 1995 sarin attack on Tokyo's subways seemed to confirm the darker view of the apocalyptians. At the direction of their very human god, Aum Shinrikyo's members fit the pattern of religious fanatics willing to kill thousands. This attack reminded us that organizations other than identified terrorist groups could carry out significant acts of terrorism. It showed that a group was capable of clandestinely acquiring and experimenting with both chemical and biological weapons for years without detection, despite numerous suspicious incidents. But the attack also demonstrated the difficulties of developing and deploying biological or chemical devices. Although it had months of experimentation and an ample budget, the Aum Shinrikyo cult developed only a crude version of nerve gas, which it dispersed in a primitive manner that reduced its effectiveness so that casualties were limited. Within weeks of the attack, Aum Shinrikyo was destroyed, its leaders under arrest. More than seven years later, no terrorist organization has yet tried to duplicate the attack.

There is no inexorable escalation from truck bombs or even suicide air attacks to WMD. Nonetheless, terrorist desires to use WMD cannot be discounted. On September 11, al Qaeda terrorists were trying to kill tens of thousands. They succeeded in killing thousands. Captured documents and interrogations of captured al Qaeda members have revealed the organization's aspirations to acquire chemical, biological, and nuclear capabilities, although there is no indication that it has such capabilities today. If it had those capabilities, al Qaeda would undoubtedly be willing to use them.

There is distance between ambition and achievement. Chemical, biological, and radiological weapons will not necessarily cause mass destruction—worst-case scenarios are planning vehicles, not forecasts. In the most plausible scenarios, the psychological effects of chemical, biological, or radiological attacks are likely to vastly exceed the actual death and destruction, but we are on the frontier of a new, more dangerous domain.

SOME REALISTIC ASSUMPTIONS

Strategy must be based upon realistic assumptions about the current situation. Al Qaeda, its associates, and its successors will fight on. It draws upon a deep reservoir of hatred and a desire for revenge, and U.S. efforts have reduced, not eliminated, its ability to mount significant terrorist operations.

It must be presumed that al Qaeda will exploit all of its ability to cause catastrophic death and destruction—there will be no self-imposed limits to its violence. Attempts to cause massive death and destruction using conventional or unconventional weapons are likely. It can also be presumed that al Qaeda will continue its efforts to acquire and use WMD; that it will attack U.S. targets abroad where possible; and that it will attempt to mount attacks within the United States. Al Qaeda constitutes the most serious immediate threat to the security of the United States.

Although some measure of success has been achieved in uncovering terrorist plots, the ability of U.S. agencies to detect and prevent future terrorist attacks is limited. There will not be sufficient intelligence to provide adequate warning in every case, and while security is being increased around likely targets of terrorist attack, terrorists can attack anything, anywhere, anytime, while it is not possible to protect everything, everywhere, all the time. Some attacks will occur.

Chapter Three

STRATEGY FOR THE SECOND PHASE OF THE WAR ON TERRORISM

The United States has formulated and carried out a coherent first-phase strategy in the war on terrorism. But what next? The campaign has now entered a more difficult phase. The greatest challenge is that as military operations move beyond a single theater, the more complex tasks will be dispersed among numerous departments, agencies, and offices, and the focus on the overall U.S. strategy will be lost, along with the nation's ability to coordinate operations. That strategy must continue to emphasize the key elements outlined below.

The destruction of al Qaeda must remain the primary aim of the American campaign. Al Qaeda will adapt to new circumstances; it may disperse, change names, merge with other entities, or be absorbed into its own successors, but as long as its leadership, structure, operatives, relationships, financing, and ability to recruit survive in any form, it will seek to repair damage, reestablish connections, issue instructions, and mobilize resources to support further terrorist operations. The al Qaeda enterprise itself cannot easily be deterred. It can be disabled only by permanently disrupting the process that provides it with human and material resources. Further terrorist attacks must be kept within the level of tolerable tragedy; another catastrophe on the scale of September 11 must not be allowed to occur.

The pursuit of al Qaeda must be single-minded and unrelenting. The episodic nature of terrorism (long periods of time elapse between major attacks), the heavy burden of security, and the public's impatience for closure can tempt the United States into dangerous complacency. Distracting events, including the conflict between Israel and the Palestinians, the confrontation between India and Pakistan over Kashmir, and America's determination to deal with other threats to national security must be addressed in the context of the immediate and continuing threat posed by al Qaeda.

The United States cannot inflict upon its dispersed and amorphous terrorist foe the immediate destruction that would serve as a deterrent to other terrorist entities contemplating alliance with it or replication of its war on America. However, assured destruction can be pursued over time—years, if necessary—without letup, without amnesty, as an ongoing reminder to others of the consequences of provoking the United States.

The campaign against terrorism will take time. Wars against terrorists throughout history have been long, even when the terrorists operate on the national territory of the government they oppose and are accessible to its authorities. Italy's Red Brigades fought from the late 1960s to the early 1980s, and after years of quiet, they may now be reemerging. Germany's Red Army Faction survived from the early 1970s to the 1990s. The Provisional Wing of the Irish Republican Army emerged in the late 1960s and laid down its arms only at the end of the 1990s. Spain's ETA is approaching its fifth decade in the field. Colombia's guerrillas can find their origins in armed struggles that began more than a half-century ago.

Al Qaeda itself represents more than a decade of organizational development built upon relationships that were first established in the 1980s. Its active planning for a terrorist war on the United States began not later than the mid-1990s, and its planning for September 11 began three or possibly four years before the actual attack, starting with plots elaborated in the first half of the 1990s. The thoroughness of al Qaeda's planning suggests that it has prepared for a long campaign, one that inevitably will involve setbacks. It is probably prepared to lie low indefinitely. The battle against al Qaeda could last decades.

The fight in Afghanistan must be continued as long as al Qaeda operatives remain in the country. There may be differences within al Qaeda between those who wish to make their last stand in

Afghanistan (and have no other options) and those who would disperse to reconstitute new versions of the organization elsewhere. Although some analysts argue that the United States has only complicated its task by chasing al Qaeda out of Afghanistan, I believe that it is preferable to destroy al Qaeda operatives in Afghanistan rather than hunting for them elsewhere. Continued pressure in Afghanistan will consume al Qaeda's resources and distract its leadership. Premature withdrawal—historically, the American tendency—would be dangerous. Only when al Qaeda is completely destroyed or when the new Afghan government can effectively exercise authority throughout its territory can withdrawal be risked.

Long-term operations in Afghanistan will require carefully controlling the application of violence in order to avoid the errors and collateral damage that will fuel Afghan hostility and pressure to depart. If Americans accept the commitment to remain in Afghanistan for a very long haul, the mode of operations can be altered to reduce the risks of counterproductive incidents. It may be prudent to place more emphasis on Special Forces operations, longer tours of duty, and the creation of specially trained combined Afghan-American hunter units. It may also be necessary to tighten the rules governing the use of American air power. With time, it will be increasingly beneficial to ensure that military successes are seen as those of Afghan warriors rather than American air power.

The continued U.S. presence in Afghanistan must not be seen as an occupation by foreign predators. Positive benefits of America's involvement—the reconstruction of infrastructure, assistance for health care and education, the restoration and preservation of Afghanistan's cultural heritage—can temper the country's natural resistance to outsiders.

Pakistan must be kept on the side of the allies in efforts to destroy the remnants of al Qaeda and the Taliban and dilute Islamic extremism. The government of Pervez Musharraf faces a potential coalition of Taliban supporters, militant Muslim groups committed to a continuation of the war in Kashmir, and Sunni extremists who for years have waged terrorist campaigns against Shi'ites and political opponents, principally in Karachi. The loss of Pakistan's support could reverse America's victory in Afghanistan. It could provide al Qaeda with a new sanctuary in the turbulent tribal frontier areas that border Afghanistan, leaving the United States and its allies with the dismal prospect of large-scale military operations in Pakistan. If a new Pakistani government were hostile to the West, the United States could find itself faced with military action against Pakistan itself. The most likely successor to the present government is not a more liberal, democratic, pro-Western regime, but one that is at the very least less accommodating. A more radical Islamic Pakistan could emerge, one that is more sympathetic to the extremists, more belligerent on the issue of Kashmir, and in possession of nuclear weapons.

The United States must be firm in ensuring that President Musharraf fulfills his pledges, especially those that involve constraining the activities of the extremists and halting infiltration into Kashmir, which could provoke a dangerous war with India. This will demand much of a weak government: that it check the activities of extremists in Pakistan and Kashmir; shut down the religious academies that feed recruits to extremist groups; cooperate with the allies in rooting out and running down al Qaeda operatives; and implement political reforms that ultimately will deliver democracy, while confronting religious extremism, sectarian violence, separatist sentiments, and hostile neighbors. The United States needs to provide political and economic support that will enable the Pakistani government to demonstrate the positive benefits of the alliance while checking popular bellicose sentiments in Kashmir. Without destabilizing the country, the United States should also try to nudge Pakistan toward the political reforms that are prerequisite to democracy and development.

New networks must be created to exploit intelligence across frontiers. Suspected al Qaeda operatives arrested worldwide since September 11 are providing some information about the terrorist network. The capture of documents found at al Qaeda safe houses and training camps will add to the picture, but this material must be effectively exploited to support the continued identification and pursuit of al Qaeda's remaining cells and the successful prosecution of those arrested. Rapid and accurate translation, analysis, and dissemination to investigators and prosecutors in the United States and abroad will require an unprecedented level of multinational coordination between intelligence services and justice departments. Magistrates and prosecutors abroad must receive intelligence in a form that is both useful and legally admissible within their varying systems of law. And the United States must understand the legal and political concerns of each of its allies and adapt its strategy accordingly. Not every suspected terrorist need be in U.S. custody, nor can information flow only in the direction of Washington.

U.S. agencies still have great difficulty sharing intelligence among themselves, although the situation is improving. Only recently have intelligence efforts and criminal investigations been orchestrated to enable successful prosecution of foreign terrorists. Achieving even better cooperation and coordination internationally will require structures that exist today only in embryonic form. It may require the creation of a U.S. task force dedicated to the coordination, collection, and dissemination of vital material to justice departments and intelligence services abroad. It may require the creation of bilateral and multilateral task forces focused on dismantling the al Qaeda network and the deployment of liaison personnel abroad for the duration of the campaign.

The crucial second phase of the war on terrorism cannot be accomplished unilaterally—international cooperation is a prerequisite for success. Full cooperation will be limited to a few governments. The British, with whom some of the mechanisms for close intelligence cooperation are already in place , will continue to be America's closest allies. NATO and other traditional allies also can be expected to cooperate closely. The cooperation of the French is especially important, although it brings with it a unique set of challenges. France has global intelligence resources, vast area knowledge, and valuable historical experience in dealing with the threat posed by terrorists operating in North Africa and the Middle East.

Russian cooperation is also important, for both political and technical reasons. Although Russian intelligence today may not match the capabilities of the Soviet intelligence infrastructure during the Cold War, and the Russian leadership tends to see terrorism exclusively through the lens of its conflict in Chechnya, Russia nonetheless has valuable knowledge and experience in Central and South Asia and can be a major contributor to ongoing international efforts to combat terrorism. Although they have significant differences in approach, Russia and the United States are natural allies on this issue.

Israel, America's closest ally in the Middle East, has vast knowledge and a strong political agenda. Historically, intelligence cooperation is close and will continue to be so, even as the two countries occasionally have differences on how to address the Palestinian issue.

Moderate Arab regimes will also contribute to the intelligence pool. Diplomacy can create new coalitions that extend beyond those of traditional allies. The United States should be flexible enough to exploit opportunities for cooperation among governments it previously has penalized for their support of terrorism. Both Libya and Sudan are anxious to normalize relations, and Sudan has offered outright cooperation in the fight against bin Laden. The United States need not seek the political endorsement of those countries on every issue, but it could be operationally and politically useful to have strong nationalist governments—even those critical of the United States— seen to be cooperating against al Qaeda's terrorism.

It is not natural for intelligence agencies to share. The CIA, with more experience in the give and take of international intelligence collection and diplomacy, is better at it than the FBI, whose organizational culture derives from the prosecution of crime. Sharing intelligence with foreign services is never easy, but unlike the Cold War era when there were understandable concerns about Soviet penetration, there is far less concern today that al Qaeda or other terrorists have burrowed into the intelligence services of America's traditional allies, and no one is concerned about keeping the terrorists' secrets. Except as intelligence-sharing is limited by the requirement to protect sources, methods, and ongoing operations, exposure rather than withholding should be the aim.

This is a war against specific terrorists—the goal is to combat terrorism. The President has said that we are at war, and the Congress has passed a joint resolution authorizing military action against al Qaeda and the Taliban as well as future actions against other nations, organizations, or persons found to have participated in the September 11 attacks. Although it may still fall short of a declaration of war, this formal expression of belligerency against terrorists and those who assist them enables the United States to more easily keep the initiative. Previous uses of military force against terrorists were limited to the framework of retaliation, although U.S. officials shunned that specific term. The United States on occasion struck back against terrorists and their state sponsors to disrupt or discourage further attacks, but the initiative remained in the hands of the terrorists. Moreover, retaliatory strikes had to be timely and seen as proportionate to the attacks that provoked them. While it might have been hoped that terrorists would fear that the United States would attack them a second time, this never happened. The President's declaration and subsequent Congressional resolution clearly signal an intent to attack terrorists whenever, wherever, and with whatever methods the United States chooses. It facilitates covert operations, and it creates a requirement for a specific plan of action.

The use of the term *war* does not carry any recognition of terrorist outlaws as *privileged combatants* entitled to treatment as prisoners of war, although, of course, the United States will not mistreat captives. It does not end American efforts to bring terrorists to justice through the legal system, either the American system or that of other countries with capable authorities who are willing to enforce the law. In countries without such authorities, the United States may take appropriate measures to defend itself. Such a declaration does not oblige the United States to run down every terrorist or attack every nation identified as a state sponsor of terrorism. Sensible diplomacy will prevail.

President Bush has correctly portrayed the war on terrorism as likely to be a long war, but it has finite aims: the removal of the Taliban government; the destruction of al Qaeda's training bases in Afghanistan; putting Osama bin Laden and his associates on the run; and rounding up al Qaeda's operatives around the world. The United States is not going to destroy every terrorist group or pursue every terrorist in the world, but as a matter of self-defense, it will wage war against terrorists capable of causing casualties on the scale of September 11. The targets are specific.

But America is not "at war" with terrorism, which is a phenomenon, not a foe. It is trying to *combat* terrorism. To make terrorism an unattractive mode of conflict, the United States will collect and exchange intelligence with allies. It will conduct criminal investigations. It will seek to expand international conventions and cooperation. It will assist in resolving conflicts that may produce terrorism and will address the causes of the deep hatred that terrorists are able to exploit. This is consistent with U.S. actions for the 30 years since the creation in 1972 of the Cabinet Committee to Combat Terrorism.

The distinction between *war* on terrorism and *combating* terrorism may also be useful in dealing with allies who attempt to enlist the United States in their wars. As counterterrorism becomes a new basis for American foreign policy, local conflicts are being presented or relabeled to enlist American political and material support. In some cases, the United States may go along in order to gain the support of other nations for its own efforts. But America is not at war with everyone's terrorists, and not all nations need be front-line participants in America's war against al Qaeda. Nevertheless, all nations should cooperate in combating terrorism, an obligation that has been formally recognized in United Nations Resolution 1373. Efforts to deal with root causes of terrorism fall under the rubric of combating terrorism, not the war against al Qaeda. Dealing with terrorist events below the threshold of catastrophe falls within the realm of combating terrorism; events above that threshold provoke war. For the foreseeable future, the United States will be dealing with both.

The current U.S. strategy should be amended to include political warfare. There appears to be a curious bias in America: The nation endorses death to terrorists but is loath to use influence. This bias has been perpetuated in bureaucratic in-fighting and deliberate misrepresentation. But it is not sufficient to merely outgun the terrorists. The enemy here is an ideology, a set of attitudes, a belief system organized into a recruiting network that will continue to replace terrorist losses unless defeated politically. At a tactical level, the campaign should include efforts to discredit al Qaeda, create discord, provoke distrust among its operatives, demoralize volunteers, and discourage recruits. At a strategic level, political warfare should be aimed at reducing the appeal of extremists, encouraging alternative views that are currently silenced by fear and hostile policy, and discouraging terrorists' use of WMD. The United States invested a great deal in this type of activity in the early years of the Cold War with some success, but its growing military superiority has led to this vital component of warfare being discarded. Changes in public attitudes and in communications technology will not permit a return to the sometimes brilliant but often risky operations of a half-century ago, nor would this be desirable. But political warfare is an arena of battle that should be subjected to rational inquiry.

Deterrent strategies may be appropriate for dealing with the terrorists' support structures. The very nature of the terrorist enterprise makes the traditional strategy of deterrence difficult to apply to terrorist groups. In traditional deterrence, the adversaries do not exceed mutually understood limits and will not employ certain weapons, although their continued existence is accepted. Deterrence worked in the Cold War, where central decisionmakers were in charge and in control on both sides. The limits and the consequences were mutually understood. Coexistence was acceptable. Deterrence regulated the conflict; it did not end the struggle.

Deterring terrorism is an entirely different matter. Here, there are diverse foes, not a single enemy with different goals and values. Terrorist leaders are not always in complete control, and they often have difficulty constraining their own followers. Coexistence is not a goal, on either side. Would the United States accept the existence of al Qaeda and any form of freedom for its current leaders, even with credible promises that they will suspend operations against this country? As individual "repentants" ready to cooperate in the destruction of the organization, perhaps; as leaders of al Qaeda, never. Nor are there any acceptable limits to continued terrorist violence.

Still, the notion of deterrence should not be too hastily abandoned. The existence of self-imposed constraints in the past—and for most groups, today—suggests decisionmaking that calculates risks and costs. Al Qaeda's unwillingness to attack Saudi targets despite its denunciation of the ruling family suggests that even bin Laden's lieutenants make political calculations. We do not know what these are or how they are weighted by the decisionmakers. Al Qaeda may be reluctant to kill fellow Arabs; or if attacked, the ruling Saudi family might push its Wahabi religious allies to denounce bin Laden—and the Saudi government does have clout in the worldwide Islamic community. Moreover, al Qaeda may deem attacking an Arab country to be inconsistent with its vision of focusing its violence on the United States. If any of these speculations is correct, then Saudi Arabia has achieved a level of deterrence. The United States may not be able (or may not want) to duplicate this situation with al Qaeda. It may prefer to demonstrate that large-scale attacks will bring unrelenting pursuit and ultimate destruction in order to deter future terrorist groups.

Deterrence might also be employed in targeting terrorists' support systems. Economic sanctions, although blunt instruments, have had some effect in modifying state behavior. The fate of the Taliban serves as a warning to state supporters of terrorism.

Financial contributors to terrorist fronts may also be deterred by threats of negative publicity, blocked investments, asset seizures, exposure to lawsuits, or merely increased scrutiny of their financial activities. Institutions that assist or tolerate terrorist recruiting may be deterred by the prospect of all members or participants coming under close surveillance. Communities supporting terrorists might be deterred by the threat of expulsions, deportations, selective suspensions of immigration and visa applications, or increased controls on remittances.

Stings may also be used as a deterrent to terrorists seeking WMD. Bogus offers of materials or expertise can be set up to identify and eliminate would-be buyers or middlemen, divert terrorists' financial resources, and provoke uncertainty in terrorists' acquisition efforts.

It must be made clear that terrorist use of WMD will bring extraordinary responses. As terrorists escalate their violence, it is necessary to create a firebreak that signals a different set of responses to terrorist attempts to use WMD. The term *weapons of mass destruction* is used deliberately, to distinguish these weapons from chemical, biological, radiological, or nuclear devices, which collectively may be referred to as *unconventional weapons.* Conventional weapons (from explosives to fully fueled airliners) may be used to create mass destruction—thousands of deaths—whereas chemical, biological, or radiological weapons may cause far less than mass destruction—12 people died in the 1995 Tokyo sarin attack, and the anthrax letters killed five people. The intent here is to focus on *mass destruction,* not *unconventional weapons,* although some ambiguity might not be unwelcome.

Even if attacks involving unconventional weapons do not result in mass casualties, their use could still cause widespread panic with enormous social and economic disruption. This would be true of radiological attacks and almost any deliberate release of a contagious disease. It is, therefore, appropriate to speak of weapons of mass effect as well as weapons of mass destruction. For purposes of response, the United States may decide to treat them as the same.

I have argued since 1977 that it should be a well-understood article of American policy that to prevent terrorist acquisition or use of WMD, the United States will take whatever measures it deems appropriate, including unilateral preemptive military action. In his speech at West Point on June 1, 2002, President Bush warned that "if we wait for threats to fully materialize, we will have waited too long." He went on to declare that the United States would take "preemptive action when necessary."

The United States may reassure its allies that preemptive action is unlikely in circumstances where local authorities have the capability of taking action themselves and can be depended upon to do so, but it is not necessary to precisely outline the circumstances in which U.S. action would be precluded. If preemptive military action is required, the government should be prepared to make a compelling public case *after the event* that such action was justified. The United States failed to do this after the American attack on Sudan in 1998. In the event of such an attack, the United States will be inclined to presume, or may choose to presume, state involvement. In a response to any terrorist attack involving WMD, all weapons may be considered legitimate.

Obviously, these warnings apply more to states than to autonomous terrorist groups who may acquire a WMD capability on their own and may find threats of possible unilateral preemption, unrelenting pursuit, and the possible use of any weapon in the U.S. arsenal to be unpersuasive. The warnings, however, may dissuade states, even hostile ones, from offering expertise or material support to terrorists moving toward WMD; such states may instead be persuaded to take steps to ensure that terrorist actions do not expose them to the danger of preemptive action or retaliation.

Another possible deterrent, perhaps more compelling to the terrorists' supporters and sympathizers than to the terrorists themselves, would be to widely publicize the fact that a major bioterrorism attack involving a highly contagious disease such as smallpox would almost certainly result in a pandemic that would spread beyond U.S. borders. Despite some weaknesses in its public health system, the United States, with its vast medical resources, would be able to cope with an outbreak, as would Europe. But with weak public health institutions and limited medical capabilities, the world's poorer nations would suffer enormously, perhaps losing significant portions of their populations. And if terrorists were to unleash some diabolically designed bug that even the United States could not cope with, the world would be doomed. This grim realization may not stop the most determined fanatic, but it may cause populations that currently find comfort in the illusion that only arrogant Americans will suffer from bioterrorism to come to the view that taboos against certain weapons are necessary to protect all.

Homeland security strategies must be developed that are both effective and efficient. The form future attacks by al Qaeda might take is impossible to predict, and areas of vulnerability both within the United States and abroad are infinite. Commercial aviation remains a preferred target for terrorists seeking high body counts; public surface transportation offers easy access and concentrations of people in contained environments; cargo containers have been identified as a means by which terrorists might clandestinely deliver weapons. Because of its size and complexity, the critical infrastructure of the United States is hard to protect; then again, terrorists have seldom attacked it, preferring instead to go after targets offering high symbolic value or killing fields. Blowing up bridges, pylons, and rail lines is more consistent with guerrilla and civil wars. Still, that does not mean that terrorists will not seek to carry out traditional sabotage in the future.

Security is costly and can be disruptive. A serious terrorist threat to the U.S. homeland may persist for years and indeed may become a fact of life in the 21st century; therefore, the security measures that are taken now will likely have to remain in place for a very long time. Terrorists are aware of the cascading economic effects of the September 11 attacks and may conclude that terrorism is an effective way of crippling America's economy.

Terrorists have learned to think strategically rather than tactically, to study and exploit specific vulnerabilities rather than to simply blast away until their opponent yields. If al Qaeda terrorists are allowed to successfully implement a strategy of economic disruption, America will lose the war. It can win only by removing the threat. But at the same time, the U.S. defense must be efficient.

It is therefore necessary not only to increase security but also to reduce the disruption that can be caused by future attacks, as well as the disruptive effects of the security measures themselves. America has just begun to formulate a homeland defense strategy. The current "castles and cops" approach may prove to be costly and disruptive. Priorities must be set. Instead of trying to protect every conceivable target against every imaginable form of attack, policymakers must explore strategies that accept a higher level of risk but offer greater strength or resiliency. The aging infrastructure may be replaced with more powerfully constructed facilities (a feature of some Cold War architecture) or with multiple facilities that provide continued service even if one goes down. This is not a new approach—terrorism simply has become a new ingredient in architecture and system design. There is ample room for research here.

The war against the terrorists at home and abroad must be conducted in a way that is consistent with American values. America cannot expect the world's applause for every action it takes in pursuit of terrorists abroad, but it is important not to squander the international support upon which the United States unavoidably will depend if it is to win the war. Military force is at times justified, but the violence should never be wanton, even if future attacks provoke American rage. The monument to those killed on September 11 and to those who may die in future terrorist attacks cannot be a mountain of innocent dead in some distant land.

At home, it is imperative that America play by the rules, although those rules may be changed. Every liberal democracy confronting terrorism has been obliged to modify rules governing intelligence collection, police powers, preventive detention, access to lawyers, or trial procedures. The United States has attempted to kill enemy commanders during times of war—the prohibition against assassination is a presidential directive, not a law. Captured terrorists may be tried in civilian courts or before military tribunals, but in either case, rules of evidence and the right to representation should apply. It is appropriate that any suspension of such rules be clearly set forth, widely discussed, and endorsed by legislation with time limits or renewal requirements to ensure that it does not become a permanent feature of the landscape. Measures that appear *ad hoc* and arbitrary should be avoided.

Finally, it is necessary to be determinedly pragmatic. America's goal is not revenge for the September 11 attacks. The goal is not even bringing individual terrorists to justice. It is the destruction of a terrorist enterprise that threatens American security.